Library Technology
REPORTS
Expert Guides to Library Systems and Services

Planning and Implementing a Sustainable Digital Preservation Program

Erin Baucom

ALA TechSource
alatechsource.org

American Library Association

Library Technology
REPORTS

ALA TechSource purchases fund advocacy, awareness, and accreditation programs for library professionals worldwide.

Volume 55, Number 6
Planning and Implementing a Sustainable Digital Preservation Program
ISBN: 978-0-8389-1819-7
DOI: https://doi.org/10.5860/ltr.55n6

American Library Association
50 East Huron St.
Chicago, IL 60611-2795 USA
alatechsource.org
800-545-2433, ext. 4299
312-944-6780
312-280-5275 (fax)

Advertising Representative
Samantha Imburgia
simburgia@ala.org
312-280-3244

Editor
Samantha Imburgia
simburgia@ala.org
312-280-3244

Copy Editor
Judith Lauber

Production
ALA Production Services

Cover Design
Alejandra Diaz and ALA Production Services

Library Technology Reports (ISSN 0024-2586) is published eight times a year (January, March, April, June, July, September, October, and December) by American Library Association, 50 E. Huron St., Chicago, IL 60611. It is managed by ALA TechSource, a unit of the publishing department of ALA. Periodical postage paid at Chicago, Illinois, and at additional mailing offices. POSTMASTER: Send address changes to Library Technology Reports, 50 E. Huron St., Chicago, IL 60611.

ALA TechSource
alatechsource.org

About the Author

Erin Baucom is an assistant professor and the digital archivist at the University of Montana. She is responsible for developing strategies, workflows, and policies for ingest, management, and preservation of born-digital materials acquired by the archives. She provides digital asset management instruction to the students, faculty, and staff of the university. She earned her master's degree in library science with a concentration in archives and records management from the University of North Carolina at Chapel Hill in 2016. She also holds a BA in history from Old Dominion University.

Abstract

More and more libraries are scaling up their digitization, digital scholarship, digital archiving, and data management programs. All of this effort could be lost to a major failure of technology, a shift in administrative priorities, or a loss of institutional memory. The loss would not be just the materials themselves, but also the resources used to build and promote these collections to users. *Library Technology Reports* (vol. 55, no. 6), "Planning and Implementing a Sustainable Digital Preservation Program," will help libraries assess their current abilities, determine what they are committed to preserving, develop administrative and technological support, and create a digital preservation program that will be sustainable through organizational and technological change.

Subscriptions
alatechsource.org/subscribe

Contents

Chapter 1

Introduction

A digital preservation program is an essential piece of your organization's total archives and preservation department. Whether your institution is a museum, a library, an archives, or even a corporation, every organization will eventually need a short-to-medium-term digital preservation program for no other reason than legal compliance. This is because many forms of digital information have no viable analog surrogate. Long-term digital preservation is the only way to maintain existing and future digital materials that organizations have invested time, money, and personnel resources in creating. Many cultural heritage materials will not exist as anything other than digital objects in the future. For all of these reasons, sustained digital preservation efforts are and will be required.

So, what is digital preservation? Digital preservation is an interlocking system of policies, workflows, technical solutions, and *good enough* efforts meant to keep digital objects authentic and usable in the long term. Digital objects are composed of bitstreams, sequences of ones and zeroes, which require specific software and hardware components to remain accessible to users. The digital objects you preserve could be born digital (those materials with no original paper counterpart) or digitized copies of analog originals. Digital material can be composed of many smaller parts that work together to form a whole. An example is the audio, moving image, and caption files that make up an accessible film. It is the goal of a digital preservation program to maintain and provide access to authentic copies of digital objects, which does not always mean that a user will experience the digital object as it was when it was created. Your organization can say that it has preserved an authentic digital object when the content, context, appearance, structure, and behavior of the digital object have been maintained even through software and hardware changes.[1]

There is no one perfect solution for creating a digital preservation program; instead, it is making an ever-evolving effort to keep up with your organization's current needs and continually planning for future circumstances. Unlike their analog counterparts, digital objects need constant monitoring and intervention to remain usable and authentic. Therefore, digital preservation program development is an iterative cycle of assessment, policy development and refinement, implementation, and maintenance. This can make digital preservation seem intimidating to those new to the practice. This intimidation and the overwhelming amount of information available on the subject of digital preservation can cause decision paralysis about where to start. This paralysis is what causes the most damage to digital objects. Doing nothing is guaranteed to cause your fragile digital objects to decay. The damage may be reversible, or it may not. The most important part of digital preservation is doing *something*. What that *something* is will depend upon the specific needs and abilities of your organization.

This leads me to my most important point about digital preservation programs. At their core, they are an exercise in risk management. You will build your entire program around what your organization determines is acceptable risk to the authenticity and usability of the digital objects in your care. The less risk you believe is acceptable, the more robust your program will be and the more resources your organization will need to assign to the program. The more risk your organization is willing to accept, the less comprehensive your program will be and the fewer resources your organization will assign to the program. It is up to you to advocate for the risk level you believe will provide authentic and usable digital objects to your users without exceeding the levels of resources assigned to your program.

Digital preservation programs require sustainable investment of financial and personnel resources. Some organizations have successfully converted short-term projects into sustained digital preservation programs. It has more often been the case that short-term projects lead to large quantities of digitized objects or specialized tools that stagnate and slowly move toward obsolescence. Before you create a large corpus of digitized materials or accept a donation with terabytes of data into your archive, advocate for the resources to set up and maintain a digital preservation program. The initial assessment process can provide you with the material to create a business case to support the continuation of digital preservation program development efforts. As Nancy McGovern emphasizes, digital preservation programs are three-legged stools that depend upon organizational infrastructure, technological infrastructure, and a resource framework.[2] Without one of these pieces, the stool cannot stand, and thus the program will not be viable. It can be surprising, once an assessment is started, to find out how many of the pieces are already in place, especially on the technology leg.

In an effort to demystify digital preservation and start your organization on the path to a viable program, I discuss in this report reliable methods, tools, and policies developed by the digital preservation community for use by digital preservation practitioners when building and maintaining their digital preservation programs. While I have written this report with new practitioners in mind, experienced practitioners may find nuggets of knowledge in the following chapters that may help them to revamp their existing systems. I deliberately chose to focus the report on technology-agnostic practices any organization can use to develop a program that fits its resources. That being said, I also provide practical strategies and tools your organization may be able to implement when assessing and implementing your digital preservation program. The tools and workflows I present in this report have been developed and maintained through a collaborative effort of the entire digital preservation community across the world, so I feel confident in their longevity and usability.

In chapter 2 of this report, I address the standards and best practices that digital preservation practitioners use to develop and maintain their programs. This is followed by chapter 3, which focuses on the assessments that you should complete before developing your digital preservation program and when your organization goes through major changes that impact your digital preservation program. The assessment chapter includes sample assessment tools and examples of how existing audit standards can be used in predevelopment decision-making efforts. Chapter 4 is about policy development. The creation and maintenance of policies is an important way to reach out to your internal and external stakeholders and collaborators to inform them about why digital preservation is important and necessary. Policy development is also a way to advocate for the resources your digital preservation program needs. Your assessments and policy documents will determine how you implement your digital preservation program. To help you leverage your assessment and policy efforts, chapter 5, on implementation, discusses a variety of workflows for the various stages of the digital preservation life cycle. The implementation chapter also covers how to maintain your digital preservation program through technological and administrative change. As you will see by the end of this report, digital preservation does not end; it only continues on in a different form into the future.

Notes

1. Thomas C. Wilson, "Rethinking Digital Preservation: Definitions, Models, and Requirements," *Digital Library Perspectives* 33, no. 2 (March 10, 2017): 128–36, https://doi.org/10.1108/DLP-08-2016-0029.
2. Nancy McGovern, Digital Preservation Management: Implementing Short-Term Strategies for Long-Term Problems website, accessed June 5, 2019, https://dpworkshop.org.

Chapter 2

Standards and Best Practices

To give you a bit of background, the basis of the way digital preservation is now practiced was developed in the 1990s and early 2000s. At that time, preservationists acknowledged that the number and variety of digital objects being created would overwhelm existing methods for managing them. To tackle this problem, multiple studies were conducted and initiatives started to address the lack of knowledge and methods to deal with these digital materials.[1] The best-known study is the 1996 *Preserving Digital Information: Report of the Task Force on Archiving of Digital Information.*[2] This report was generated by a task force created by the Commission on Preservation and Access (CPA) and the Research Libraries Group (RLG). The task force was charged to investigate contemporary roadblocks preventing the preservation of digital objects and to make recommendations on how to overcome these problems. One of the essential practices used in digital preservation programs today, engaging digital content creators as early as possible in the life of a digital object, was a result of this report. This practice includes educating creators on the long-term needs of digital objects—not just the technical needs, but also the need for contextual information to remain with the digital materials. This contextual information allows future users to interpret the original intentions of the creator and provides provenance that helps to boost the trustworthiness and authenticity of the objects.

There are a few ways for you to integrate this education into your organization's culture. The first is through a records management approach, where you require your content creators to use a limited set of software products for their tasks, mandating what format files will be saved in, requiring a specific folder and file structure with strict naming conventions, and so forth. This type of approach requires you to constantly communicate with, and in some cases supervise, your content creators. Many organizations are not able to allocate the resources necessary for this kind of oversight, and it usually works only for internally produced content. Another approach is to work with creators at the point of content transfer. You could go through a standardized checklist with your creator to gain the essential contextual pieces needed to provide provenance and descriptive information to future users. This approach also allows you to limit the types of files your organization will receive by requiring content creators to migrate the files into standard, open source file formats before the transfer can be completed. You can add another layer to this *upon transfer* approach by providing education sessions to creators in your organization or to potential donors in the community you are trying to cultivate. This instruction can include recommendations for file formats, file-naming conventions, and tips for organization so that the transfer process, when it eventually occurs, goes more smoothly.

Preserving Digital Information had another pivotal recommendation—that a certification program for digital repositories be created so a network of trusted digital archives could be established. This recommendation led to two foundational international standards that the digital preservation community still relies upon today: the Open Archival Information System (OAIS) model and the Trustworthy Repositories Audit and Certification (TRAC) checklist.[3]

The OAIS model is a foundational document that digital preservationists use to discuss the nuts and bolts of a digital preservation repository. OAIS, ISO 14721:2012, was developed by the Consultative Committee for Space Data Systems (CCSDS) because the space industry produces an enormous amount of data that it is required by law to preserve and provide access to.[4] The industry initially had no formalized plan for this data. The CCSDS realized at the outset that this standard would eventually be used beyond space data systems and that, even within its own industry, there was a tremendous variation in systems and technology. This led the CCSDS to develop the standard to be applicable across many different disciplines with many different technology requirements, using language that is intentionally vague as to how to implement the standard. This approach makes the document extremely difficult to understand. In brief, OAIS describes an archival repository as a system that encompasses end-user needs, administrative oversight, the process by which digital materials become fully preserved and usable collections, and the foundational concept of packaging contextual information (metadata) with the digital objects throughout the entire process.[5]

To help you and other digital preservationists accomplish the goal of creating and maintaining a successful archival repository, OAIS defines several mandatory responsibilities for every digital preservation program. These responsibilities include what many archivists would consider basic practices of appraisal, arrangement and description, collection development policies, and access requirements. The appraisal requirements, for instance, specify that you have a donation agreement that defines what content is being transferred to the repository and the intellectual rights associated with the content, with particular emphasis on how intellectual rights intersect with preservation responsibilities.[6]

The arrangement and description aspects of the mandatory responsibilities require that you provide enough contextual information for the users to be able to independently discover and access all the content of the archive. To make digital content usable, you will often need to change the format or structure of the digital object. How the original document was formatted and structured is an essential piece of contextual information that needs to be recorded, as is the description of any changes you make. These arrangement and description responsibilities can be the most resource-intensive piece of the OAIS requirements, personnel-wise. With regard to collection development, OAIS requires that your digital archives program define who your end users are and what your users need from your archival repository. This will drive which kinds of digital objects you collect and how you preserve them.[7]

Finally, the access requirements, like the arrangement and description responsibilities, are more technology-focused than in traditional archival repositories, but with a similar emphasis on provenance and authenticity. Your digital archives program must have transparent policies and procedures to guarantee the long-term preservation of and access to your digital objects. Further, digital objects should be easy for your users to find. They should be provided to your users in a reliable manner, where the digital object provided to the user is an exact copy of the original the digital object in your repository or, if that is not possible, a copy of the original digital object in an updated format (also known as a *migrated* or *transformed* digital object) for the user to access. If you provide an updated copy of the digital object, you should have available to your users an easy-to-understand audit trail that clearly indicates when the digital object was transformed, why it was transformed, how it was transformed, and who did the work.[8]

Beyond these mandatory responsibilities, OAIS also defines a model for building a digital preservation repository.[9] This model defines a set of functions for how digital content is packaged and moved through a digital repository from content creator to end user and how the digital content is preserved over the long term. These functions include ingest, archival storage, data management, access, preservation planning, and administration. The first function, ingest, is a series of processes that define how a repository receives a Submission Information Package (SIP) from the content creator, how it validates that the transfer from the creator is uncorrupted and complete, how the SIP is transformed into an Archival Information Package (AIP), and how the AIP is transferred into preservation storage. The archival storage function includes more than the technology that stores the digital objects. It ensures that the digital content is unaltered (authentic) and readable in the long term. The archival storage function also emphasizes how important it is to monitor your preservation storage and plan for disasters. The next function, data management, is focused on the creation of, discoverability of, and documentation of the descriptive, preservation, and administrative metadata associated with your digital objects in your preservation system. The preservation planning function requires that your digital preservation program constantly monitor the digital preservation landscape, prepare for and implement changes as needed to keep your digital repository functional, and comply with international standards and best practices. The access function focuses on how users find and retrieve digital objects from your digital archive. Finally, the administration function defines how the day-to-day management of your digital preservation program is done.[10] All of these functions can be developed in stages and then woven together to form the whole. You do not have to plan your program to be a fully compliant OAIS repository from the start. Instead, you should decide which function you are able to build out first and plan for that, leaving yourself the ability to integrate each new function together as you build them.

I place so much emphasis in this chapter on learning the OAIS standard because it is the common language that digital preservation professionals use to discuss repository development and maintenance with each other and with the information technology professionals who build and implement these systems. OAIS will soon be up for review, and it has been suggested that the wider digital preservation community, beyond the Consultative Committee for Space Data Systems, be allowed to suggest updates to make the standard easier to read and more directly applicable to how repositories are currently functioning.[11]

Digital repository developers needed an actionable way to answer the question "Is our repository OAIS-compliant?" For this, another ISO standard was created: 16363, Audit and Certification of Trustworthy Digital Repositories.[12] The development of this standard started when a working group comprised of members from the Research Libraries Group and the Online Computer Library Center authored a report in 2002, *Trusted Digital Repositories: Attributes and Responsibilities*, which defined a trusted digital repository and recommended that there be a continued push for digital archives certification programs.[13] The report provided other high-level recommendations about where more research was needed to refine digital preservation implementation strategies. The Research Library Group first partnered with the National Archives and Records Administration in 2003, and later with the Center for Research Libraries in 2005, to operationalize the recommendations from *Trusted Digital Repositories: Attributes and Responsibilities*. These efforts resulted in the Trustworthy Repositories Audit and Certification (TRAC) checklist, published in 2007.[14] This checklist was used as the basis for ISO Standard 16363 which is one of the certification methods used to determine a Trustworthy Digital Repository.[15]

While ISO 16363 is the formal standard, many digital preservation programs use the original 2007 TRAC report as a planning, self-assessment, and external evaluation tool instead of going through the formal certification process.[16] TRAC was created through an international effort with contributors from different types of organizations that have a stake in the standards by which digital preservation programs are judged as consistent with recommended practice. These organizations included many entities beyond those that would traditionally be considered archival institutions, such as data repositories and research communities. This is an acknowledgement of the fact that digital preservation is most successful when content creators are involved with the effort as early as possible.

The TRAC document is an essential assessment tool because it emphasizes all aspects of a digital preservation program: technical setup, administrative policies and procedures, financial sustainability, and more. These aspects are split into three categories: organizational infrastructure, digital object management, and infrastructure and security risk management. This tool can be intimidating to first-time users due to its length and jargon-heavy language. The document was written with an assumption that the audience consists of professionals already familiar with digital preservation practice. However, each requirement is broken down into small, bite-sized pieces with suggestions for how the repository can demonstrate achievement. The document was intentionally developed to be flexible so that it could be used by many different types of institutions. The document emphasizes that the assessment of an institution should be based upon that institution's "mission, priorities, and stated commitments."[17] A caveat to this is that "regardless of the size, scope, or nature of the digital preservation program, a trusted repository must demonstrate an explicit, tangible, and long-term commitment to compliance with prevailing standards, policies, and practices."[18]

There is a simpler, easier-to-understand certification process called the CoreTrustSeal, which has been specifically developed for data repositories.[19] New digital preservation programs can use the requirements for planning purposes, and existing repositories can use the certification as a self-assessment tool. While TRAC has over one hundred requirements, the CoreTrustSeal has sixteen. The language of the CoreTrustSeal is data-focused, but by replacing the word *data* with *content* or *digital objects*, it is easy to see how these same requirements can be used to evaluate a digital preservation program. This certification program requires documentation of policies, procedures, licenses, and plans be publicly available when possible in an effort to promote transparency in how data repositories are set up and run. This transparency is an essential part of how a repository is deemed trustworthy.

OAIS, TRAC, and CoreTrustSeal emphasize the importance of documentation for a digital preservation system. Part of this documentation is the metadata associated with digital content, often grouped into four categories: descriptive, administrative, technical, and structural. Descriptive metadata is information about the digital objects; administrative metadata is information about rights, provenance, and a preservation audit trail; technical metadata is information about how to access the digital objects; and structural metadata is information about how digital objects relate to each other when they belong to a set.[20] Practically, these categories often overlap—one piece of metadata may fit into one or all of these categories at once. OAIS specifically requires metadata in the form of Preservation Description Information (PDI), which should include provenance, reference, fixity, contextual, and access rights information, all which contributes to maintaining a digital object's authenticity and therefore could be considered administrative metadata.[21] In practical terms, there are two metadata standards that are essential to the preservation of and access to digital materials: Preservation Metadata: Implementation Strategies (PREMIS) and Metadata Encoding and Transmission Standard (METS), both maintained by the Library of Congress.

PREMIS was originally a working group formed

by the Online Computer Library Center (OCLC) and the Research Libraries Group in 2003 created to build upon the report *A Metadata Framework to Support the Preservation of Digital Objects,* written by the Preservation Metadata Framework working group in 2002.[22] The report proposed thirty metadata elements that the PREMIS working group used to create a data dictionary and a set of XML schemas for implementing the dictionary in digital preservation systems. The PREMIS Data Dictionary focuses on developing and maintaining preservation metadata as a means of keeping digital objects viable, usable, understandable, and authentic.[23] The working group that developed PREMIS required most of the core metadata to be generated and processed automatically by the repository system. Like OAIS, the PREMIS Data Dictionary is meant to be implementation-agnostic. Therefore, the way each digital preservation program produces and analyzes PREMIS metadata can be unique. A repository can comply with PREMIS without using the XML schemas provided by the PREMIS working group to create the information. As long as a repository can export its preservation metadata and crosswalk it to the Data Dictionary, that repository is considered PREMIS-compliant. Most importantly, the PREMIS Data Dictionary was developed to be OAIS-compliant so that all metadata generated to comply with the PREMIS standard will also comply with OAIS PDI requirements.[24]

METS was originally developed for cataloging digital library objects. Its purpose is to extend descriptive metadata to include structural metadata that describes the organization of the component parts of an object. METS also allows descriptive metadata to be enriched with technical metadata describing the software and hardware information relevant to the digital object and, when necessary, the digitization specifications for a digital object. The Digital Library Federation provided an XML document format for encoding METS information. This XML document format allows repositories to point to descriptive metadata and administrative metadata listed in an externally maintained system like an EAD finding aid or a MARC record so that these efforts do not have to be duplicated, saving valuable time and resources. One of the unique aspects of the METS document is the hierarchical map that links elements of the structure to content files and their associated metadata. The METS document also includes a behavior section that can associate executable actions with the content. While METS was originally created for digitized images in an online library platform, it has been modified and extended over the years to meet the needs of digital preservation programs.[25] Like PREMIS, there are tools available that can automatically generate METS metadata and package that metadata with the digital content to form OAIS information packages.

These standards, together with others not mentioned here, create digital preservation best practice. In fact, since the early 2000s, when these standards were initially created, few new standards have been developed. Instead, the digital preservation community has focused on the practical implementations of these abstract reference models. These collaborative efforts have led to multiple case studies and templates being made available to the existing and new members of the digital preservation community to help develop new programs and boost existing programs to the next level. Institutions that have resources to devote to the actualization effort, working in concert, have developed tools and repository systems for their own use and then made these available to the community as a whole to benefit smaller organizations. These standards can be intimidating, but implementing best practice to conform to the standards is possible. I will discuss how in the following chapters of this report.

Notes

1. Erin Baucom, "A Brief History of Digital Preservation," in *Digital Preservation in Libraries: Preparing for a Sustainable Future*, ed. Jeremy Myntti and Jessalyn Zoom (Chicago: American Library Association, 2019), 3–19.
2. Donald Walters and John Garrett, *Preserving Digital Information: Report of the Task Force on Archiving of Digital Information* (Washington, DC: Commission on Preservation and Access, 1996), ERIC, https://eric.ed.gov/?id=ED395602.
3. Baucom, "A Brief History of Digital Preservation," 5–6.
4. International Organization for Standardization, *Space Data and Information Transfer Systems – Open Archival Information System (OAIS) – Reference Model,* ISO 14721:2012 (Geneva, Switzerland: ISO, approved March 2003; reaffirmed September 2012).
5. Brian Lavoie, *The Open Archival Information System (OAIS) Reference Model: Introductory Guide*, 2nd ed., DPC Technology Watch Series (Glasgow, Scotland: Digital Preservation Coalition, October 1, 2014), https://doi.org/10.7207/twr14-02.
6. International Federation of Film Archives, "Digital Preservation Principles," accessed June 5, 2019, https://www.fiafnet.org/images/tinyUpload/E-Resources/Commission-And-PIP-Resources/TC_resources/Digital%20Preservation%20Principles%20v2%200.pdf.
7. International Federation of Film Archives, "Digital Preservation Principles."
8. International Federation of Film Archives, "Digital Preservation Principles."
9. For a visual representation of information packages moving through the functional entities of the OAIS reference model, see National Archives of Australia, figure 2 in "Digital Preservation Policy," February 20, 2018, www.naa.gov.au/about-us/organisation/accountability/operations-and-preservation/digital-preservation-policy.aspx.

10. International Federation of Film Archives, “Digital Preservation Principles.”
11. Thomas C. Wilson, “Rethinking Digital Preservation: Definitions, Models, and Requirements,” *Digital Library Perspectives* 33, no. 2 (March 10, 2017): 128–36, https://doi.org/10.1108/DLP-08-2016-0029.
12. International Organization for Standardization, *Space Data and Information Transfer Systems – Audit and Certification of Trustworthy Digital Repositories*, ISO 16363:2012 (Geneva, Switzerland: ISO, approved February 2012).
13. Research Libraries Group and Online Computer Library Center, *Trusted Digital Repositories: Attributes and Responsibilities* (Mountain View, CA: RLG, May 2002).
14. 14. “Trustworthy Repositories Audit and Certification: Criteria and Checklist, version 1.0,” RLG—National Archives and Records Administration Digital Repository Certification Task Force (Chicago: Center for Research Libraries and Dublin, OH: OCLC, February 2007), https://www.crl.edu/sites/default/files/d6/attachments/pages/trac_0.pdf.
15. Baucom, “A Brief History of Digital Preservation,” 7–8.
16. *Trustworthy Repositories Audit and Certification: Criteria and Checklist*, version 1.0, RLG—National Archives and Records Administration Digital Repository Certification Task Force (Chicago: Center for Research Libraries and Dublin, OH: OCLC, February 2007), https://www.crl.edu/sites/default/files/d6/attachments/pages/trac_0.pdf.
17. *Trustworthy Repositories Audit and Certification*, 9.
18. *Trustworthy Repositories Audit and Certification*, 10.
19. CoreTrustSeal, “Core Trustworthy Data Repositories Requirements,” v01.00, November 2016, https://www.coretrustseal.org/wp-content/uploads/2017/01/Core_Trustworthy_Data_Repositories_Requirements_01_00.pdf.
20. Edward M. Corrado and Heather Lea Moulaison, *Digital Preservation for Libraries, Archives, and Museums* (Lanham, MD: Rowman and Littlefield, 2014), 113-115.
21. Corrado and Moulaison, *Digital Preservation for Libraries, Archives, and Museums*, 127-131.
22. OCLC/RLG Working Group on Preservation Metadata, *A Metadata Framework to Support the Preservation of Digital Objects* (Dublin, OH: OCLC, June 2002), https://www.oclc.org/content/dam/research/activities/pmwg/pm_framework.pdf.
23. “PREMIS Data Dictionary for Preservation Metadata, Version 3.0,” PREMIS Preservation Metadata Maintenance Activity website, Library of Congress, December 14, 2018, http://www.loc.gov/standards/premis/v3/index.html.
24. Priscilla Caplan, *Understanding PREMIS*, revised by PREMIS Editorial Committee (Washington, DC: Library of Congress, 2009, rev. 2017), www.loc.gov/standards/premis/understanding-premis-rev2017.pdf.
25. “METS: An Overview and Tutorial,” Metadata Encoding and Transmission Standard (METS) website, Library of Congress, March 30, 2017, www.loc.gov/standards/mets/METSOverview.v2.html.

Chapter 3

Assessment

Your institution or organization may have already begun digital preservation efforts without knowingly advancing a digital preservation program. These efforts most commonly occur unintentionally in policy development or technological systems improvements. For instance, your collection development policies, mission statements, and access procedures could already mention digital materials. Your technology systems administrators often have already started along the road of information security, systems diversity, and more. Without a comprehensive assessment of your organization, there is no way to tell what, if any, digital objects your institution currently maintains, what resources your organization has to devote to the project, and what policies or procedures already exist that could help or hinder preservation efforts. Therefore, the first step for any new program or even an overhaul of an existing program is to do an assessment.

There are several stages of assessment to prepare for creating or updating a digital preservation program. The first stage is getting an overview of the current digital objects that need preservation in your organization. Not all digital objects created or held by your organization are worthy of expending resources to preserve. This is similar to the fact that not every piece of paper in the world is worthy of being arranged, described, and maintained in a traditional archival repository. The second stage is to determine what resources your organization has to preserve these digital objects. The assessment of available resources should include personnel, technological infrastructure, and monetary assets. The third stage is to survey the current policies and procedures of your organization that may relate tangentially or directly to future digital preservation efforts. Finally, your assessment should conclude with the development of realistic and aspirational goals for your organization's digital preservation program. These goals will set the stage for policy creation and advocacy efforts focused on preserving existing funding and support potential increases in resources for your digital preservation program.

The first stage in your suite of assessments is to do an inventory of your institution's current digital holdings. This inventory can be as high level as listing categories of digital objects only, or as granular as listing every piece of digital media in your archives, all of the accessions with digital materials, and all of the e-journals, databases, and e-books the library has purchased or subscribes to. Most likely your inventory will land somewhere between the two extremes. Figure 3.1 is an example of this. The purpose of the inventory is to determine what you need to preserve, if anything. In the unlikely event that there are no digital objects in your holdings at present, the inventory is a place to speculate on the digital material you would like to collect from potential donors or the digital material you would like to create or capture through digitization, digital scholarship projects, or the course of regular business. What you have, or will have, in terms of digital objects will determine the procedures you create and the tools you will use in your digital preservation program.

The inventory process is an ideal time to set up and implement your first workflow for your digital preservation program. In many organizations, digital media is separated out from the original donation during the accession and appraisal process. There are organizations that have discontinued the practice of separating materials in different formats—photographs, for example—to different storage locations in a repository because of newer archival processing guidelines like "More Product, Less Process."[1] Separation is still a necessary strategy for digital media due to the fragility of the digital carrier media. Also, separation allows you to prioritize the stabilization of digital materials as they arrive at your archives. The stabilization process will be covered in chapter 5.

The separation and inventory workflow I use starts upon finding a digital media object, such as a CD, DVD, flash drive, or floppy disk, in an accession.

	Number of								
Accession Number	**5.25 Floppy Disks**	**3.5 Floppy Disk**	**CDs**	**DVDs**	**Flash Drives**	**Hard Drives**	**Network Transfer**	**Email Attachments**	**Total**

Figure 3.1
Sample digital object inventory. This table is a sample inventory document that can be used when assessing what digital objects your organization currently holds or might like to preserve in the future.

I immediately remove the item and place a flag or separation sheet in the place I found the item in the box or folder. The separation sheet includes the date of separation, the type of item, a description of the item, where the item has been moved to, and who performed the separation. The description of the item includes some kind of digital object identifier in case there are multiple digital media items in an accession. The identifier I assign to the digital media in the University of Montana's archival collections is AccessionNumber_ObjectNumber, where the object number starts at 001. (You may have collections that have more than 100 digital media items, so plan ahead for this when numbering.) It is important to label the digital media in some way with that identifier as well. The "moved to" location should be a centralized location where you keep all digital media. All digital media objects that belong to the same accession should be kept together, either in a folder for a few objects, or in their own box for many objects, clearly labeled with the accession number.

The next stage in your assessment is to identify and document all the resources available to perform digital preservation activities. This part of the assessment will require that you connect with other people in your organization and discuss current and potential resources that could be assigned to a digital preservation program. It is important that you have a simple explanation ready of what digital preservation is and in what context you are asking these questions to create a common understanding of what you are trying to achieve. This is crucial for when you interact with your information technology professionals. They will use terms similar to those used by a digital preservationist, but the working definitions of those terms can be very different for the two fields. Other colleagues may not have any idea what digital preservation is or why you are asking for more information about resource allocation. An example of a simple, focused pitch about what you are doing and why would be: "I am trying to find out how the library *backs up* internally produced content to see how often we *archive* our content, how long that content stays in storage, and in how many different places the content is saved to determine how secure our digital content is for future use. Can you help me?" This is a long question with many pieces, but it is focused on specific aspects of digital preservation: storage diversity, length of storage time, and how often backups are overwritten. Simply asking the question will help you start the discussion about a digital preservation program with colleagues in your organization.

The most important resource to assess is personnel because personnel time tends to be the most heavily expended resource for any digital preservation program. Are there currently members of your organization who have digital preservation responsibilities as part of their job descriptions? If so, who are they, and how much time can they spend on the effort? The amount of current knowledge and available time personnel can spend on the digital preservation program will drive your implementation strategy. A successful digital preservation program could be one full-time person with a high level of knowledge working on the program with support from the information technology department and the bibliographic management department on occasion. Another successful approach could be one or two people from every department with a medium amount of digital preservation knowledge working on the program as they can. These are just two of many potential scenarios. The key is that whatever personnel time and expertise allocation you develop remains sustainable in the long term. The size of your organization will determine how granular this part of the assessment will be. The intent is to determine if your organization *has* these resources. A potential way to document this assessment is by using your institution's organizational chart. List your potential collaborators by job title, and document, for each person, if they are willing to contribute to the program, and if so, how much time would they be able to spend on it and what skills they believe would be useful to a digital preservation program. In this way, you can map out the current abilities of your collaborators, whether additional training may be needed, and the amount of participation you can expect from your collaborators in helping you plan your digital preservation program implementation strategies.

The assessment of available resources continues with an inventory of your organization's current technology resources and standard practices. One of the best tools for this type of assessment in the National Digital Stewardship Alliance's Levels of Preservation.[2] The Levels of Preservation are currently undergoing a scheduled revision to bring the text up-to-date with current practice and to make the document more relatable to practitioners new to the field and collaborators whose main area of expertise may not be archives. The structure of the document—"a tiered set of guidelines and practices intended to offer clear, baseline instructions on preserving digital content at four progressive levels . . . across . . . different functional areas . . . focused on specific preservation actions"—will remain the same.[3] The emphasis in the Levels of Preservation is on activities, but by determining what activities you have completed, you can also make an inference about what technology resources you currently have available. If you do the assessment with a colleague knowledgeable about your technology resources, your colleague may be able to suggest resources that are available but not currently utilized for digital preservation.

Finally, you will need to determine and document what financial resources, beyond personnel time and existing technological infrastructure expenditures, are available to fund your digital preservation program. Do not be discouraged if the answer is none. When starting a digital preservation program, it is more important to have personnel and technological resources available because so much of digital preservation is in planning, policy setting, and workflow creation using existing resources. When your program has been up and running for a while, you will have a better understanding of the gaps in your digital preservation system and then be able to request specific funds to fill those gaps and have evidence to support your funding requests.

The next stage in your assessment is to look at your organization's mission, policies, and procedures. This survey should be done with an eye toward where a digital preservation program will support the mission or fill gaps in existing collection development policies, access policies, and so on. If existing procedures or workflows in the organization produce digital materials, those may need to be integrated into the new digital preservation program. For example, if your organization is creating permanent born-digital records, you need to know where those records are, how they are being saved in the short term, and what kinds of electronic formats they are being saved in so that you will have a better understanding of the preservation needs of the records. Similarly, if your organization is already creating digital surrogates of analog materials, you will need to understand how that process works, what the final formats of those digital copies will be, and if your organization intends to invest in preserving the digital copies over time.

Having completed all of your assessments, it is time to develop two sets of goals. The focus of the goals should be to advance your digital preservation program toward sustainability and further compliance with the standards I talked about in chapter 2. One way to create your goals is to map your assessments to one of the certification checklists or to the Digital Preservation Capability Maturity Model (DPCMM).[4] For those just starting out, I suggest mapping to the DPCMM because it has only fifteen areas of performance, each explicitly requiring conformance to OAIS requirements, versus the one hundred plus requirements in TRAC or the data-specific nature of the CoreTrustSeal.

A capability maturity model, the heart of how the DPCMM is structured, is "a set of structured levels that describe how well the practices, processes and behavior of an organization can [reliably] and sustainably produce desired outcomes . . . [using] a series of associated activities and baseline metrics used to measure performance in a given area."[5] The DPCMM used the OAIS and TRAC ISO standards (14721 and 16363 respectively) to develop the performance measures for each of the fifteen areas. For each area, a digital preservation program can fall between Level 0 (nominal) and Level 4 (Optimal). There is a break between Levels 2 and 3 that requires the digital preservation program must fully conform to ISO 14721 in a sustained manner before Level 3 can be achieved. The fifteen areas are broken into two sections, Digital Preservation Infrastructure, which speaks to organizational commitment, and Digital Preservation Services, the processes required to actively preserve digital material. Using the Digital Preservation Capability Self-Assessment Scorecard, you can map your assessment results to the DPCMM and receive a scorecard with an overall score of the stage of your digital preservation program.[6] Figure 3.2 is an example of a final scorecard. The Digital Preservation Capability Self-Assessment Scorecard was originally created and structured for records managers, so you will have to be a little flexible when answering the questions if that is not your institutional context.

You can now, using this map from assessment to requirements, set goals for raising your capability level in those areas you deem most necessary and most achievable with your current resources. This could be a set of fifteen goals, or it could be set of four, depending on your organization's particular needs and abilities. Sustainable digital preservation programs require a balance between organizational infrastructure, technological infrastructure, and sufficient resources. When you are creating your goals, make sure to not emphasize one of the areas over the others. If you already have sufficient technology to meet your current needs, focus on goals that improve organizational policies and resource allocation. Digital preservation is all about how much risk you are willing to accept to your digital materials. If you are willing to accept a high level of risk, that willingness will be reflected in fewer technological goals. If you are willing to accept only a very low level of risk, then you will have a high number of technological goals.

When setting each goal, define a clear metric or set of metrics that, when achieved, will prove that the goal has been met. For example, if one of your goals is to go from DPCMM Level 0 (no access to digital preservation expertise) in Technical Expertise to Level 1 (minimal access to expertise), your metric could be to have one or more employees successfully complete a set of digital preservation courses.[7] These goals and metrics will become the road map you use to create your digital preservation program implementation plan. The DPCMM maturity stages are cumulative. You do not truly move up a stage until you are able to implement and sustain all of the requirements of the lower stages. To truly build a sustainable program and to get the most out of the DPCMM as an assessment tool, I suggest your goals reflect moving all of the DPCMM categories to the same level. If some of your categories are at Level 0 and some are at Level 1, an achievable goal would be to move every category into Level 1 and sustain your abilities at Level 1 for a period of time before trying to move any of your categories to Level 2.[8]

The second set of goals will differ from your first set only in that you are creating aspirational goals. If you had more people, more time, and more money, what would be your ideal goal for each requirement and its associated metrics for achievement? It may not be achieving a Level 4 for every requirement. Remember, your digital preservation program needs to work for your organization and your community of users. This may mean a less complicated and less resource-intensive program than the ideal espoused by TRAC, the CoreTrustSeal, or the DPCMM. Instead, your aspirational goal may be that you meet the requirements for an end-to-end system where *all* digital content is being preserved and users have a path to independently access that content. This would mean that your goals are to achieve the minimum necessary for preservation but the maximum necessary for access. Another organization may put more time and resources into the preservation end because its policies require long-term restrictions on content before users are able to access the materials. In this case, the preservation piece is much more intensive because it is more difficult to recognize a possible preservation

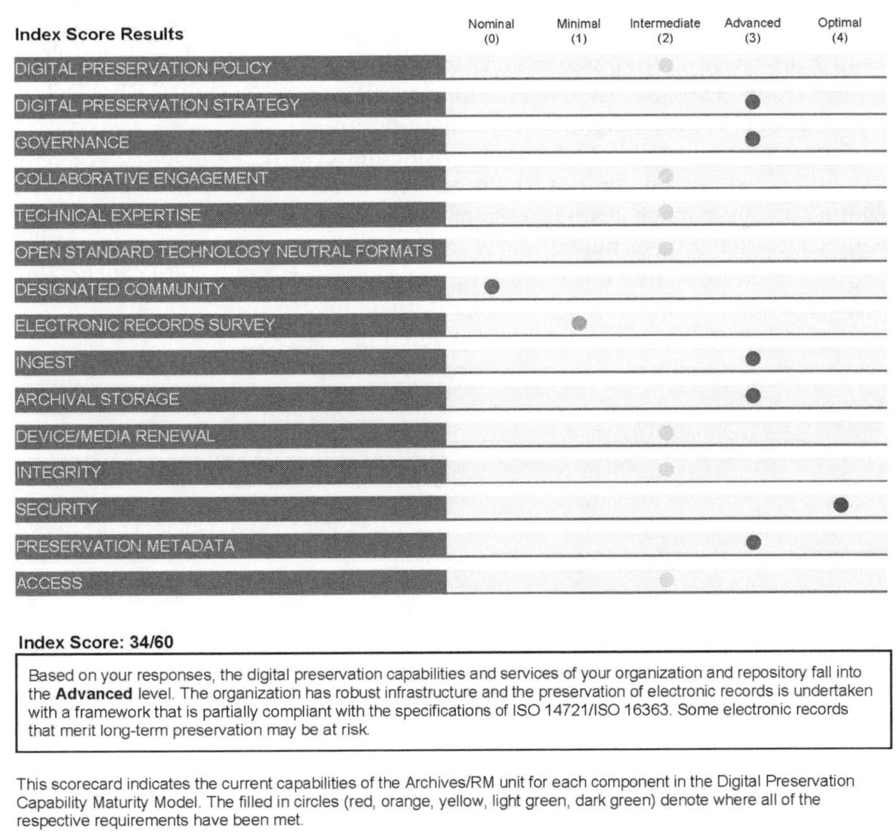

Figure 3.2
Sample Digital Preservation Capability Self-Assessment Scorecard. This is an example of a completed scorecard with the fifteen areas of performance individually scored and an overall score for the entire program.

problem when materials are not being constantly accessed.

Your aspirational goals will set the stage for how you decide to advocate for your digital preservation program in the future. These goals and metrics will help you plan for future expansions to your digital preservation program. This plan will help you create an advocacy campaign to request new resources for your program. You can go to your organizational leaders with evidence of what you have already done and a plan for where the new resources will be expended with potential outcomes already laid out. You can also use your assessment of the organization's mission and goals to show where the digital preservation program supports your organization's leaders' initiatives and plans for the overall organization. Your assessments and goals can also help you determine where collaborations with other organizations will be most beneficial and effective, especially if other organizations that you routinely work with have done a similar assessment. In fact, I encourage you to do these assessments at the same time as your partner organizations because you can benefit from the lessons others in your group learn from internal discussions with information technology groups and resource allocators in their own institutions. Common goals that result from these shared assessments may allow you to pool resources with other institutions to fill common gaps in everyone's digital preservation program.

This is something that I have done with other academic libraries in the state of Montana. We worked together using a much leaner version of the assessment series that I have talked about in this chapter. We have been focusing on building the knowledge of member librarians and slowly increasing their organizational infrastructure to the point where they can request support for a digital preservation program. The result of the common assessment was a common need for digital preservation policies at every institution, either new or an updated version. This is the next step in creating a sustainable digital preservation program, and thus the next chapter of this report.

Notes

1. Mark Greene and Dennis Meissner, "More Product, Less Process: Revamping Traditional Archival Processing," *American Archivist* 68, no. 2 (Fall/Winter 2005): 208–63, https://doi.org/10.17723/aarc.68.2.c741823776k65863.
2. Megan Phillips, Jefferson Bailey, Andrea Goethals, and Trevor Owens, "The NDSA Levels of Digital Preservation: An Explanation and Uses," Library of Congress, 2013, www.digitalpreservation.gov/documents/NDSA_Levels_Archiving_2013.pdf.
3. Phillips et al., "The NDSA Levels," 1.
4. Charles Dollar and Lori Ashley, *Digital Preservation Capability Maturity Model (DPCMM)*, v. 2.7 (San Francisco: Tournesol Consulting, July 6, 2015), www.securelyrooted.com/dpcmm, under "DCPMM Background and Performance Metrics v2.7."
5. Dollar and Ashley, *Digital Preservation Capability Maturity Model*, 8.
6. The Digital Preservation Capability Self-Assessment Scorecard is a service that you will need to register for and requires that you begin your self-assessment within seventy-two hours of registering. You may reregister at any time (DigitalOK login page, accessed June 5, 2019, www.digitalok.org); Dollar and Ashley, *Digital Preservation Capability Maturity Model*.
7. Dollar and Ashley, *Digital Preservation Capability Maturity Model*, 20.
8. Dollar and Ashley, *Digital Preservation Capability Maturity Model*, 8.

Chapter 4

Policy Writing and Engaging Stakeholders

After completing your assessment and setting your goals, it is time to write a digital preservation policy. Depending on where you are in your journey toward a sustainable digital preservation program, just beginning or several cycles of maintenance in, you will have a more or less detailed policy. Your digital preservation policy document should affirm your organization's commitment to a digital preservation program and provide an avenue by which to create a business case for your creating or improving your digital preservation program. This document is not about implementation, so it will not be necessary to go into detail about how you will accomplish your digital preservation goals.

A successful digital preservation policy will consider your organization's institutional context. Write your policy to mirror your organization's strategic priorities and goals. Include the language of your organization's mission and strategic plan to link the policy to your leadership's agendas. You need to remember when writing your policy that this document will be read by multiple audiences, including internal departmental or unit stakeholders, organizational leadership, partner institutions, and potential and existing donors. With this audience diversity, it is important to keep the language of the policy high level, with limited jargon, and the length relatively short.

At the most basic level, your policy should have three sections:

1. Rationale—Why you have a digital preservation program.
2. Scope—Not only what you hope to preserve but also what is beyond your ability and desire to preserve. Your scope section should also include a definition of what your organization considers a "record" or the "original" to be. Depending on your organization, the legal definition of a record in your area may be what you use. In other cases, it may be an institutional definition of what constitutes an "original copy" that provides a transparent explanation of what *original* means in a digital context where everything is technically a copy.
3. Roles and Responsibilities—Those positions, departments, and units that will be participating in the digital preservation program and how they will be contributing.

It is possible, and in some cases necessary, that your policy will be only three paragraphs long, one paragraph each for rationale, scope, and roles and responsibilities. Ideally, these sections will be the main headings under which you organize the document, with each subsection describing in plain language more granular aspects of your current or proposed digital preservation program. The following policy outline is based on Daniel Noonan's "Digital Preservation Policy Framework: A Case Study":[1]

Digital Preservation Policy Outline

- *Summary:* The summary is the very first section in the policy and should be no more than two or three sentences long. It should state what the digital preservation program does and why the program is important at an organizational level.
- *Rationale:* The rationale section is the high-level heading that covers why your organization should have a digital preservation program. According to how complex your policy is, this may simply be a header, or it could be the entire *why* section of the document. However, either in one large text block or in smaller subsections, this part of your policy should include purpose, mandate, objectives, principles, and challenges.
    - *Purpose:* Purpose is a single sentence that provides your reader with a clear statement of what the digital preservation policy is meant to do for your organization.
    - *Mandate:* Depending on the complexity of

your organization and where the digital preservation program lives in the institution's hierarchy, the mandate section will either be department/ unit-focused or institution/ organization-focused. The mandate addresses the legal, institutional, and unit requirements for preserving digital objects. If your institution is small enough that you are writing the mandate section with an institution or organization focus, it will also cover a description of the intentions of your organization's digital preservation program, and you will not have an objectives section. Be sure to include parts of your institution's mission statement verbatim and then provide a direct link to how digital preservation helps the organization meet its mission.

- *Objectives:* If your organization is large enough that you wrote the mandate section from a department or unit perspective, your mandate will include only a statement that addresses legal and organization-imposed requirements for preserving digital materials. The objectives section will be separate and describe the intentions of an organization's digital preservation program. This is, again, where the institution's mission statement should be included in some way to clearly display that the digital preservation program is an essential component of meeting the institution's larger goals.
- *Principles:* The principles section, like rationale, can be one section or several subsections depending on your audience. This section is important because it allows you to directly address your organization's values and how the digital preservation program will operate according to those values. This section also allows you to connect your digital preservation program to international standards and best practices. Some possible subsections include *sustainability, collection management, technical infrastructure, preservation activities,* and *metadata.*
    - The *sustainability* subsection makes clear that your organization is committing to the long-term funding required to keep a digital preservation program running. This subsection can also be where you include how collaboration efforts between organizations to pool preservation resources can help to support long-term preservation efforts.
    - The *collection management* subsection addresses how your organization will follow standards and best practices for creating, receiving, processing, and providing access to authentic digital materials. If you have internally produced content that will be included in your digital preservation program, the collection management subsection could include a statement about your digital preservation program's commitment to working with internal content creators to have them create digital materials in a digitally sustainable manner.
    - In the *technical infrastructure* subsection, you acknowledge, at a high level, the importance in investing in technology for the preservation of digital materials and the fact that your organization is committed to making this investment not just initially, but in an ongoing manner. As with all other aspects of this document, this will be specific to your organization. Your technology commitment could be an investment in internal hardware systems, or it could be an investment in storage as a service.
    - The *preservation activities* subsection includes broad statements about what the preservation program does, with an emphasis on these actions being tested, evidence-based, and documented.
    - Finally, the *metadata* subsection acknowledges that digital preservation has unique metadata creation requirements and that your organization is committed to creating and maintaining this specialized metadata.
- *Challenges:* Digital preservation is an exercise in risk management. There are no guarantees, only carefully managed workflows that are intended to prevent as much loss as possible and to allow users to access the informational content of digital materials well into the future. When possible, the look and feel of the original digital objects should also be made available to users. The challenges section of your digital preservation policy should cover the risks unique to your organizational context and how the digital preservation program will address these risks. Depending on the maturity of your program, your policy may very well not have a way to address all of the risks associated with digital preservation in your organization. In those cases, acknowledging that the risks exist and that your program is not developed enough to meet the risks effectively yet is a viable approach to this part of the policy.

• *Scope:* The scope section is the second *absolute* requirement for a digital preservation policy. I have found that it is easiest to have two clear lists in this section: collection content covered by the digital preservation policy and collection content not covered by the policy. This clearly lays out to your stakeholders what you are and are not committing resources to preserving.

Your organization's collection development policy should drive what digital materials are included in the scope of your preservation program. Remember, metadata created during the digital preservation process is also digital material and therefore should be explicitly included in the scope section of your digital preservation policy. When listing what is and is not included your program, use categories of digital materials: published digital collections, unpublished digital collections, research data, administrative records, digitized collections, and so on. Those categories will make more sense to your stakeholders than more granular statements about file format types. There are two additional subsections that could be included in your scope section: *selection and acquisition* and *access and use*.

  - *Selection and Acquisition:* The selection and acquisition subsection covers how and why you acquire those digital materials within the scope of your digital preservation policy. Generally, it will include a link to your organization's collection development policy.
  - *Access and Use:* The access and use subsection describes how your organization deals with who has access to your collection materials and how materials may be used, with a specific emphasis on intellectual property rights.

- *Roles and Responsibilities:* The roles and responsibilities section is the final required section in your digital preservation policy. This is where you will list who is responsible for the digital preservation program and what those responsibilities are. The roles should be either position titles or the names of departments and units so that the policy has continuity even as specific people join and leave your organization.

When writing your digital preservation policy, include those people and departments that will be doing the actual work of digital preservation so that you all agree to the high-level commitments and goals the policy is enumerating. That way, there are no surprises later when you are asking for help developing an implementation plan or actually doing the work of digital preservation. Working on the policy together is also a way to build internal knowledge of and support for the digital preservation program so that your colleagues can become advocates for digital preservation to others in your organization.

Engaging Stakeholders

There are five major categories of stakeholders who are crucial to a digital preservation program's success: resource allocators and institutional leadership, content creators, internal collaborators, external collaborators, and end users. Often, the same person will be a part of multiple stakeholder categories. In those cases, craft your argument toward the stakeholder category that has the most sway with that person in the moment. You can use some common talking points to engage and inform all of these groups and some slightly more focused strategies for resource allocators and institutional leadership and content creators.

By this point you should have already engaged your internal collaborators through the assessment and policy-writing processes. Your external collaborators, in most cases, already believe that digital preservation is important and necessary because they are developing and implementing their own digital preservation programs. Finally, your end users provide the evidence of *use*, which is one of the critical assessment measures resource allocators require when evaluating how successful a program is. Another piece of the assessment puzzle provided by end users is qualitative evaluations of the final product of your digital preservation system—access to the digital content. If end users have a positive experience and are willing to communicate this to leadership, your users can become some of your strongest advocates for sustaining your program. This is especially true if you make clear to your users that the materials are available in part due to digital preservation efforts. This can best be accomplished with your common strategy *elevator pitch*.

At work, my title is Digital Archivist, and very few people I interact with outside of the cultural heritage sector fully understand what an archivist is, much less a digital archivist. I rarely have more than a minute to provide a coherent explanation of what digital preservation is and why it is important. In this type of situation, it helps to have a prepared set of talking points, or an elevator pitch, that can be relatable for any type of audience. This pitch needs to be short, to the point, with little professional jargon, using examples of digital content that everyone can relate to. While the examples provided in this report assume knowledge of archival practice, not all audiences will have this knowledge. When you are talking to an audience unfamiliar with archival practice, you will first need to describe what an archivist does. Without the contextual piece of what an archivist does, any discussion of digital preservation will rarely make sense. What follows are some suggested talking points that you can use to develop your own elevator pitch. There are many more examples in the Digital Preservation Coalition's "Executive Guide on Digital Preservation."[2]

- Digital preservation is a never-ending effort to maintain access to digital materials over time.
- Digital preservation requires careful planning because, as computers change, so do the ways you access older content.

- Digital preservation is *not* digitization. If you digitize something, that digital object will, in most cases, become something to preserve.
- Digital preservation involves more than a few backup copies of your digital content because, over time, those backups will no longer work with more advanced computers currently being developed.
- Digital preservation is a necessity, not a luxury, because it helps to prevent deliberate and accidental loss of digital content over time.
- Digital preservation allows you to view older versions of websites and websites that have been deleted.
- At this moment, artists are creating works that are digital only. For you to be able to experience this art in the future, digital preservation is essential.
- Digital preservation is a critical safeguard for the digital-only reports and data you are required by law to maintain.

While the elevator pitch will get you started talking about digital preservation, more in-depth conversations are necessary to achieve the kind of support required for a sustainable digital preservation program. One of the most effective ways to gain and maintain this support from your organization's leaders is through presenting a business case for digital preservation. Depending on where you are in developing your digital preservation program, this business case may be more or less formal. The document should address how digital preservation benefits your organization beyond the tried-and-true arguments of ongoing access to content. I suggest putting particular emphasis on the return on investment supplied by digital preservation programs through cost efficiencies, such as new storage mechanisms and centralized workflows for processing and providing access to digital content. You can include examples of how digital preservation reduces the risk of litigation and can support grant applications because a data management plan is now required by many funding institutions, and what is data management but another aspect of digital preservation?[3]

After you have provided these arguments as to how a digital preservation program can improve your organization, suggest specific scenarios of how you would like to implement or improve your digital preservation program. It is important to include multiple potential strategies for your digital preservation program in the document so that your leadership can better understand the different risks, resource needs, and benefits associated with different levels of digital preservation. You should always include the baseline level of no digital preservation program so that your organization's leaders can fully understand and compare the risks and benefits of having a minimal digital preservation program against not having one at all. The other options you provide should address the specific needs of your organization and the goals you defined for your digital preservation program determined by the assessments I discussed in chapter 3. If one of your strategies is to suggest building your digital preservation program in an iterative way, make sure to emphasize that the first stage of the program is not a pilot. A digital preservation program cannot be effective as a series of project cycles. It requires a sustained allocation of resources for the potential benefits you discuss in your business case to become reality.[4]

After you have developed your business case, carefully consider the best time to present it to leadership. The most impactful time to make the case for a new digital preservation program or an upgrade to an existing program is before a major changes occurs or after a catastrophic event. These situations present you with the perfect answer to "Why a digital preservation program *now*?" If your organization is preparing to relocate to a new building or introduce new technology, if a major change is forthcoming in regulations, and so on, you can craft your argument to include digital preservation in the changes already being planned. If your organization has just experienced a major data breach or has been fined for noncompliance, you can introduce a digital preservation program as a way to prevent these things from happening again. If none of these situations are likely to occur soon, one other major aspect of timing is to ask for resources for a digital preservation program when leadership is starting to plan a new budget so that you can start negotiating with leadership as part of the regular budgeting process. You may have to delay your presentation of your business case to leadership if your organization is not in the position to support a digital preservation program. In this situation, it is still important to maintain a business case that you can present when the time is right. The Digital Preservation Coalition provides a *Digital Preservation Business Case Toolkit*, which is a great resource that will guide you step by step through the process and has a template you can use when writing your own business case.[5]

The other major category of stakeholder for whom you need to tailor your digital preservation discussions is your content creators. You will have internal content creators who produce organizational materials that will eventually need to be preserved and external content creators who donate materials to you for preservation and access. To support digital preservation becoming embedded into your organization, the key is to constantly communicate with and provide training for your internal content creators. Training these content creators on what types of file formats to use, how to name and organize their files, and to add contextual information within files and folders whenever possible makes for a more efficient transfer and processing of these files when it is time for the materials to be moved into the digital preservation system. For external content creators, you could provide community trainings similar to those you provide for your organization's content creators and have online guides available for them to access, but it is more likely that you will communicate with these external donors only at the point of transfer, not at the point of creation. The next chapter will go into detail about how to tease out the vital contextual and technical information a donor can provide to you at the point of transfer.

Notes

1. Daniel Noonan, "Digital Preservation Policy Framework: A Case Study," *EDUCAUSE Review*, July 28, 2014, https://er.educause.edu/articles/2014/7/digital-preservation-policy-framework-a-case-study.
2. Digital Preservation Coalition, "Executive Guide on Digital Preservation," licensed under the Open Government License v3.0, accessed June 5, 2019, https://www.dpconline.org/our-work/dpeg-home.
3. Charles Dollar and Lori Ashley, *Digital Preservation Capability Maturity Model (DPCMM)*, v. 2.7 (San Francisco: Tournesol Consulting, July 6, 2015), 35–36, www.securelyrooted.com/dpcmm, under "DCPMM Background and Performance Metrics v2.7."
4. Dollar and Ashley, *Digital Preservation Capability Maturity Model*, 35–36.
5. *Digital Preservation Business Case Toolkit*, v. 1.1, SPRUCE Project, May 2014, Digital Preservation Coalition Wiki, http://wiki.dpconline.org/index.php?title=Digital_Preservation_Business_Case_Toolkit.

Chapter 5

Planning and Implementation

By this time you will have done an assessment of what you need to preserve and your available resources, developed goals for your digital preservation program, written a digital preservation policy, and engaged your stakeholders to get the program off the ground. Now you need to decide how to implement a digital preservation program that meets your institution's needs but is also within your organization's abilities to develop and sustain. A common reference for planning a digital preservation program is the digital curation life cycle model (figure 5.1).

The Digital Curation Centre (DCC) Curation Lifecyle Model introduces a visualization of the concept that digital preservation is an iterative process that builds, changes, and improves through each cycle of maintenance.[1] The core of the model, which is a series of concentric circles, is what the preservation program is trying to protect and provide access to, the information packages of digital content and metadata. Moving outward from the center, the model introduces the staged manner in which practitioners should approach building a preservation program. Before anything else and throughout the entire life of the preservation program, preservation planning is paramount. The next level out is community watch and participation, which is an integral piece of preservation planning. Moving further away from the center, the model provides the first level of granularity, where curation and preservation become distinct parts of the preservation program. Finally, curation and preservation are broken down into actionable and sequential stages of a preservation program. The parts of the model that are not in the circle are actions that occur only after a triggering event, such as a change to collection development policy that would require you to determine if some of the materials maintained by your digital preservation program may no longer be within the scope of your collection. Another triggering event may be that you have a large collection of photographs in a format that is no longer accessible. This would require you to migrate the data into a new format so that you can provide uninterrupted access of the material to your users.

When using the life cycle model to plan your digital preservation program, there are two common pathways to follow. The first pathway is to decide that you would prefer to subscribe to an out-of-the-box digital preservation vendor that provides a system that covers all aspects of the preservation life cycle from "create or receive" to "transform." There are several of these vendors on the market, with about an even split of proprietary systems and hosted solutions that package together open-source tools and preservation storage systems. The other pathway to designing your digital preservation program is to develop your own system, using a series of open-source and commercial tools. Which pathway you choose will depend on the resources you have available in your organization and how far along you are in your preservation program.

The benefits of the vendor solutions are that you will only need to learn how to use one software system that integrates all aspects of the preservation life cycle and that the system is maintained and updated by an external party. If your personnel resources and expertise are limited, this is a great solution to implementing an efficient and sustainable program. These solutions can be expensive, and, depending on the size of your organization, duplicate systems may already be available and implemented by your information technology department (particularly storage systems). Like other specialized systems, proprietary vendor solutions are a small market, and it could be difficult to replace one if something goes wrong or to exit from one if you are unsatisfied with its services.[2]

The second pathway toward building a digital preservation program allows you complete flexibility and the ability to build your system one piece at a time as your resources for and knowledge about digital preservation increases. Due to the foundational values of digital preservation being sustainability and collaboration, most of the necessary tools for building and maintaining a digital preservation program are open-source and are maintained by a dedicated community of practitioners. It is entirely possible to build a digital preservation program using only free, open-source tools, but that requires that you have someone on staff who has the time to devote to the program and who has a high level of technology competency.

The Preserving Digital Objects with Restricted Resources (Digital POWRR) project created a tool grid in 2013 that compared digital preservation tools using categories drawn from the OAIS Reference Model. This grid has not been updated since it was created, but it provides a snapshot of the most commonly used digital preservation tools and their suitability for different aspects of the digital preservation life cycle. The most up-to-date listing of tools is the Community Owned Digital Preservation Tool Registry (COPTR), which has recently added a subsite of Community Owned Workflows (COW).[3] These resources are essential when initially planning your digital preservation program because they can save you time. The comparison between different tools has already been done, and all you have to decide is which tools work best for your particular situation.

Before implementing your digital preservation program, either a full end-to-end system or a patchwork of tools and services, decide on who will have the authority to access and, when necessary, modify your digital content at each stage of the preservation life cycle. Establishing a transparent, trustworthy, and secure digital preservation program requires a clear set of authority controls—who has permission to read, write, modify, and delete digital content in your preservation system. In the beginning stages of the preservation life cycle, very few people should have access to the content to prevent accidental or malicious alterations. As the materials move through the preservation workflow, there will be two sets of permissions needed—one set for users accessing the fully arranged and described content, and one set for those managing the digital preservation master files, or archival information packages.[4] The permissions for researchers will depend upon the collection and your institution's rules. There are specialty repository systems, such as Mukurtu, where access restrictions can be set to conform to cultural practice.[5] The permissions for the preservation masters should be limited to the specific person or people in your information technology division and the archivists responsible for maintaining your digital preservation program. Also, in the case of the preservation masters, you should have clear guidelines that state *when* it is permissible to access these masters and for what purposes. The key to a trusted digital preservation program is transparency and consistency. Whatever pathway you take, document all of your workflows and procedures, consistently perform procedures as documented, and record any changes you make to your workflows, including why the changes were made, when, and by whom.

The digital preservation program that I manage is based upon the second pathway, a series of workflows using open-source and commercial tools and systems. The overall flow of the program is stabilize; appraise, arrange, and describe; ingest; access. This is a little different from the digital curation life cycle model's stages of create or receive; appraise and select; ingest; preservation action; store; access, use, and reuse; and transform.[6] That model is an ideal, and in practice some of the actions, such as store, are part of the entire process and not a distinct stage. As long as your program implementation is based on standards and best practice and works within your organizational context, your digital preservation program will be successful.

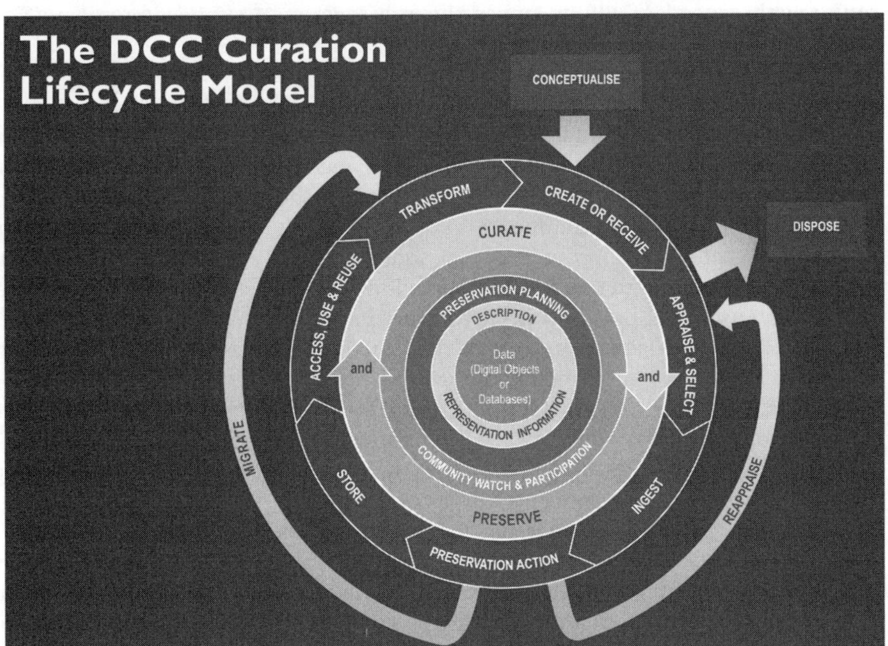

Figure 5.1
The digital curation life cycle model. Source: Digital Curation Centre, "DCC Curation Lifecycle Model," accessed June 5, 2019, www.dcc.ac.uk/resources/curation-lifecycle-model. CC BY 4.0 (https://creativecommons.org/licenses/by/4.0/#). Image has been cropped.

The rest of this chapter will present a sample implementation strategy using open-source and proprietary tools. To be able to carry out the program as outlined requires a few pieces of hardware. The first is a computer with enough memory and processing power to use the digital preservation software tools. This computer, ideally, will rarely be connected to the internet in an effort to reduce the possibility of viruses being introduced to the computer and therefore to any digital materials being stabilized or processed on the computer. The second category of hardware are internal or external drives that allow you to access the various digital media items in your collection, such as a 3.5-inch floppy disc drive, a CD/DVD drive, and so forth. Lastly, you need some form of write blocker (hardware or software) that prevents you from inadvertently changing the metadata and digital content that you are trying to preserve. The sample strategy will not include storage recommendations because storage solutions need to be tailored to your specific needs, and there is excellent existing documentation and guidance already available for building preservation storage solutions.[7]

Accession

During the accessioning process, when you are discussing what will be donated to your organization and how, digital content requires you to deviate slightly from standard practice. First, it is advisable to modify your existing deed of gift to cover the preservation needs of the digital objects you will be receiving and the potential privacy breaches that can occur when the materials are stabilized. If one of your donors wishes to retain the rights to the intellectual property of the digital materials he or she is donating, you will need to negotiate the right to preserve these materials into the donor agreement. I also recommend that you include a section in your deed of gift that requires donors to give explicit permission for digital forensics activities, which enables donors to put limits on what your organization can and cannot do with the results of those activities. In an effort to support these choices, I suggest including a predetermined list of possible restrictions and redaction options. This additional section helps you to start the conversation about what you, as the processing archivist, or a very savvy potential user could find with access to a donor's digital materials so that donors have full knowledge of what they are agreeing to.

After you have negotiated with the donor over what will be donated and what you are allowed to do with the donation, ask the donor about the digital materials he or she is going to give you. I recommend you have a template checklist with all the potential questions for any kind of digital materials donation, and then you can tailor this template for each donor, subtracting those questions that do not apply. This checklist is most effective when you are able to sit down with donors and view the potential materials they would like to donate. That way you can go through the checklist and do a preliminary appraisal of the donation at the same time. You can also glean vital contextual clues about the organization of the digital materials and ask donors questions about why they chose to do things a certain way.[8] The answers to these questions will inform the arrangement decisions you make later on. You can also make suggestions to the donor about additional organization and potential migration from unique file formats to more common file types before the transfer to your institution occurs. Finally, you can decide how the digital content will be transferred from the donor to your organization, whether through digital media or through file transfer protocols.

If the digital materials are coming to you from inside your organization, you can bypass some steps. Instead of a donor agreement with a negotiation over intellectual property and informed consent, you have a transfer agreement that provides you with contextual information similar to the information you would receive from the donor checklist. The transfer agreement should also have instructions for internal personnel that describes how the digital content should be sent to you. It is important to include the transfer instructions because it is at the point of transfer where the digital content is extremely vulnerable to loss, of both intellectual content and technical metadata. Providing a strict procedure describing how transfers are supposed to occur can help reduce these risks.

Stabilize

Stabilization is the most important step of the entire process. Ideally, this will be done as soon as you receive digital material through an email attachment, on a flash drive, on a CD, and so forth. Stabilizing your digital content means that you are establishing a record of who you received the material from, in what condition it arrived, and the original metadata associated with the material (as best as you are able) and also establishing a baseline against which you will check, through time, to see if the digital material is ever modified in a way that affects its authenticity. After stabilization, you can safely let the digital materials sit in a monitored archival storage system until you have the time to finish the process. Throughout the entire procedure you should be documenting the actions you take for each file transfer or digital media transfer, either in your accession record or in a separate digital content log. This documentation should include the following information for each transfer or digital media item:

- Accession number
- Digital object identifier/transfer identifier

- Transfer type
- Date acquired
- Who donated the transfer
- Who received the transfer
- Media (if it came on digital media): format, manufacturer, model, age, condition, media label text
- Disk image (if a disk image is created): date created, disk image filename, disk image software used, notes, files exported (Y/N)
- Stabilization: virus scan (Y/N), checksums generated (Y/N), file format report generated (Y/N), personally identifiable information scanned for (Y/N), files moved to preservation storage (Y/N), notes
- Produce AIP: AIP created (Y/N), AIP saved in preservation storage (Y/N), date of transfer to storage, network storage location, notes

As early as you can in the stabilization workflow, ideally while the digital materials are still with the creator, but definitely before you transfer the files into your digital preservation processing system, run a virus check on the digital content being transferred. Your organization should be using some kind of virus protection software. Included in these software packages should be the ability to scan for viruses. I work almost exclusively in a Windows environment, so all I have to do is right-click on the directory I want to scan, chose the virus checker, and let it run. If your organization's software does not allow this, there are some open-source virus checkers available, or your information technology professionals may suggest one that they would prefer you use. In the event that a virus or malware is found in the material, contact your information technology department to see how they would like you to proceed. If you are working in a small shop, with no support from an IT department, put the files in quarantine and try again in ninety days after your virus protection software updates with all the new patches. In this case, quarantine may mean leaving the files on their digital media carriers or refusing to accept a file transfer. Depending on your virus protection software, it may take care of the entire quarantine and remediation process for you.

After virus checking, I recommend you set up a folder directory for the accession. The highest folder in the hierarchy should be named with the accession number. Within that, if you are going to create disk images, you will have three folders: disk_image, files, and metadata. If you don't create disk images, you will have only a files folder and a metadata folder. Within the disk_image and files folder, each individual transfer, digital media or otherwise, will get a folder named with the digital object identifier. In my case, the digital object identifier is the accession number and then a number starting at 001 and going up for however many digital media objects or file transfers are in the accession. As you move through the stabilization process, transfer files and save metadata into this folder structure. Example of a folder structure:

- 🗀 2007_038
  - 🗀 2007_038_disk_image
    - 🗀 2007_038_001_disk_image
    - 🗀 2007_038_002_disk_image
  - 🗀 2007_038_files
    - 🗀 2007_038_001_files
    - 🗀 2007_038_002_files
  - 🗀 2007_038_metdata

Now you are ready to transfer your digital materials to your digital preservation processing environment. If the transfer of digital content comes on digital media, you have two choices. You can create a disk image of the digital media, or you can do a direct copy of the files from the digital media to your digital preservation processing computer. Whether or not you create a disk image will be a matter of policy, donor agreement, and type of digital media. For instance, if I receive digital content on a flash drive or an optical disk, I very rarely create a disk image because the return on investment for these digital media does not often play out in my favor. If I receive a computer hard drive, I am much more likely to create a disk image because there is so much contextual information that can be retrieved and the potential for emulation. If the digital content does not come to you via digital media, your only option is via direct copying. If you decide to create a disk image, BitCurator is an open-source, community-supported software environment that has tools for creating, documenting, processing, and viewing disk images.[9]

The vast majority of the digital content transfers I facilitate are done by direct copy mechanisms. There are two tools that I recommend for this process, DataAccessioner and TeraCopy.[10] DataAccessioner allows you to supply metadata at the point of transfer for the accession, produces PREMIS metadata after running the File Information Tool Set (FITS) on the files, checks the fixity of files after they have been moved from the original source location into your processing environment, and does not alter the files' original metadata, such as last date modified or date of creation.[11] TeraCopy has free and for-purchase versions. The free version that I use will copy files without altering their internal metadata and performs a fixity check to make sure the files were not altered upon transfer.

After the files have been transferred or the disk image created and the files exported from the disk image for the entire accession, I suggest you create a file format report that is easy to read. This report serves two purposes: it is a record of the file formats in the accession so you can determine early on if special actions will be necessary immediately or in the near future to maintain access to these files and if you need to research special software to gain access to the files. There a few different open-source tools available to do this job. You can compare them using POWRR Tool Grid or COPTR to find the one that works best for your organization.[12] I suggest that if the tool has a proprietary file format, you export the results as a comma-separated value (.csv) file type. A .csv opens well in many different spreadsheet and database software products.

The final step in the stabilization process is finding and documenting personally identifiable information (PII) and, for disk images only, extracting file system metadata. The BitCurator Environment includes the Bulk Extractor tool, which is what I use to do this. Bulk Extractor works for disk images and file sets. It generates reports on possible instances of PII and has a viewing tool that points you to where the PII is. If you have a disk image, I strongly encourage you to use the various reporting tools available in the BitCurator Environment to generate as much information about the original file system as possible.[13] At this point, you have a few choices. You can transfer the file directory for the accession into preservation storage as is until you have time to arrange and describe the files. You can make the file directory into a Submission Information Package and ingest it into your repository. Finally, you can go straight into appraising, arranging, and describing the content of the accession.

Appraise, Arrange, and Package

The appraise, arrange, and package step is very similar to the traditional version of archival processing when an archivist goes through the collection and determines what to keep, introduces a new arrangement for the files when necessary, and starts the process of creating an official description of the collection. One of the major differences between an analog collection and a digital collection is that digital collections can contain an exponentially higher number of individual "files" to go through, so you need different tools to get the job done.

I have found in practice, for hybrid collections, that you should process the analog materials before the digital. In this way, you get a feel for the creator's organizational style and start to have an idea of what you might find in the digital files. In some cases, your digital files will integrate seamlessly into your arrangement of the physical files, so each series, subseries, and so on will be a mix of physical and digital files. In other cases, you will have a series that is just computer files, but it is difficult to decide which way to go without having processed the physical materials. Processing the physical files will also help with the deduplication process.

My first step in appraisal of the digital content in an accession is to look at a visualization of the content. The two tools I use to do this are WinDirStat and TreeSize.[14] I use WinDirStat to get a quick overview of the different types of files in the accession or as a teaching tool to help internal content creators understand what they are producing and how to find out what is taking up all of their computer's memory. More often, I use the professional version of TreeSize. Not only does it show me a visual representation of the different types of file formats in a collection, but it also contains tools for deduplication of files and for finding and removing temporary files, internet files, and more. This can dramatically reduce the number of files I will eventually need to arrange.

At this point you can choose to leave the files as they are, or you can go further in the arrangement of the files. What you do will be determined by your organization's processing workflow because the decision-making factors for digital materials at this point are rarely different from those for physical materials. Generally, when I make the decision to not keep the original arrangement of digital files, it means that I am matching the arrangement of the physical files or that the collection has no discernable useful organization and therefore it would be too difficult for users to navigate in its original state. If you decide to arrange the files into a new folder structure, I recommend that you create the new folder structure first and then move the files into it. At this point you may also be renaming files individually, but this is not necessary.

After you have settled on the final arrangement of the files, you can either use a series of tools to, at the bare minimum, strip file names of special characters and normalize files for preservation and access, or you can use a tool like Archivematica, which will automate the SIP to AIP and DIP process for you.[15] Archivematica uses a series of customizable microservices that document your digital collections, perform preservation actions such as assigning a unique identifier to each digital file, remove special characters from file names, and so much more. Archivematica will also and transform the files into preservation and access versions of the original digital files when it is able to do so. You can either pay for a hosted version of the software or try and maintain your own instance of the software. Be aware that in practice Archivematica takes a lot of technical knowledge and can require a lot of maintenance. Archivematica can integrate into ArchivesSpace, Archivists' Toolkit, AToM, DSpace, or your own preservation storage. If you do not use Archivematica, there are a series of automated file renaming, file migration and normalization, and packaging tools on COPTR for you to use. From here, you can move your AIPs into preservation storage and your DIPs into your access storage environment.

A final piece of the preservation puzzle is fixity monitoring. It is not enough to create checksums of all of your digital materials upon transfer. You also need to check to make sure that each checksum does not change over time due to an accident, malicious activity, or simple bit rot. It is impossible to do this by eye, especially if your program includes millions of files. Instead, I recommend that you use fixity monitoring software that will run on a schedule and notify you of any changes. It is possible that your information technology department already uses such a service. If so, communicate with them to get access to the fixity report. If not, COPTR has a couple of options of open-source fixity monitoring tools for you to choose from.

Access

Access to digital collections for your users may take many different avenues depending on your institution's resources. It is just as valid to have users request access to the digital materials in a collection as described in your finding aid and provide them with a link to a shared folder through an online drop box as it is for users to have immediate access to digital content through a digital library or repository system. In some cases, users may access your content only from a reading room computer. The most likely solution is a combination of all of these, depending on your resources and the specific restrictions, if they exist, for each collection. What is essential is that users *have* access and there be clear documentation describing how users may or may not gain access to collections and why. At the bare minimum, a fully processed digital collection will have a finding aid or catalog record with information about how to request access to the materials.

Maintenance

An essential piece of digital preservation program implementation is maintenance. As a digital preservation practitioner, you should try to pay attention to the wider world of digital preservation literature and tool development. As new tools and services become available, evaluate them against what you are already doing. If they are an improvement, determine if your current resources would allow you to integrate a new tool or service into your existing system. If not, it may be time to create an updated business case to ask your organization's leaders for additional resources. Another part of maintenance is planning for the inevitable replacement of your existing software and hardware solutions. Hopefully, some of the burden of replacement will be shared by your information technology division. If you do not have an information technology division, it may be better to plan for a transition into storage as a service, such as cloud storage, so that you do not have to maintain your own storage infrastructure. Finally, do your own personal maintenance—attend digital preservation conferences, workshops, and webinars when you are able to. By increasing your own knowledge of digital preservation, you will create more efficient workflows and be able to modify existing tools so they work better for your organization. You will also become a stronger advocate for your digital preservation program and be better able to introduce and maintain collaborations with other digital preservation programs.

Notes

1. Digital Curation Centre, "DCC Curation Lifecycle Model," accessed June 5, 2019, www.dcc.ac.uk/resources/curation-lifecycle-model.
2. Example end-to-end preservation systems include Preservica (https://preservica.com/) and Ex Libris Rosetta (https://www.proquest.com/products-services/Ex-Libris-Rosetta.html).
3. "Tool Grid," Digital POWRR: Digital Preservation Research, 2013, https://digitalpowrr.niu.edu/digital-preservation-101/tool-grid/; COPTR homepage, accessed June 5, 2019, http://coptr.digipres.org/Main_Page.
4. Brian Lavoie, *The Open Archival Information System (OAIS) Reference Model: Introductory Guide*, 2nd ed., DPC Technology Watch Series (Glasgow, Scotland: Digital Preservation Coalition, October 1, 2014), https://doi.org/10.7207/twr14-02.
5. Mukurtu CMS homepage, accessed June 6, 2019, http://mukurtu.org.
6. Digital Curation Centre, "DCC Curation Lifecycle Model."
7. Christopher J. Prom, Erin O'Meara, and Kate Stratton, *Digital Preservation Essentials* (Chicago: Society of American Archivists, 2016); Digital Preservation Coalition, "Digital Preservation Handbook," 2015, https://www.dpconline.org/handbook.
8. Melissa Watterworth Batt, "Donor Survey DRAFT," Electronic Records Committee, Congressional Papers Section, Society of American Archivists, October 31, 2012, https://cprerc.files.wordpress.com/2015/08/sample-donor-survey_dodd-center_draft.pdf.
9. BitCurator homepage, accessed June 6, 2019, http://bitcurator.net.
10. DataAccessioner homepage, accessed June 6, 2019, http://dataaccessioner.org; "TeraCopy for Windows," Code Sector, accessed June 6, 2019, https://www.codesector.com/teracopy.
11. FITS is a tool developed and maintained by Harvard that "identifies, validates and extracts technical metadata for a wide range of file formats." File Information Tool Set (FITS) homepage, accessed June 6, 2019, https://projects.iq.harvard.edu/fits/home.
12. "Tool Grid"; COPTR homepage.
13. BitCurator homepage.
14. WinDirStat homepage, last updated November 12, 2018, https://windirstat.net; TreeSize Professional webpage, JAM Software, accessed June, 21, 2019, https://www.jam-software.com/treesize.
15. Archivematica homepage, accessed June 6, 2019, https://www.archivematica.org/en.

Chapter 6

Conclusion

Over time, work to embed your digital preservation program into your organization through training, shared services, and clear demonstrations to leadership of why the program is valuable. This will help you insulate the program from being drastically affected by institutional change. When leadership changes, overall organizational resources grow or diminish, or services are discontinued, your digital preservation program will be affected. Having clearly established policies and procedures, along with leadership's support, will help to limit the adverse effects of these changes and boost your ability to request more resources as they become available. It is always important to plan for the worst case scenario. If, at any point, you no longer have the ability to maintain your program, you should have a clear exit strategy in place.

When planning for a total dissolution of your digital preservation program, you may need to consider internally produced digital materials and digital materials donated by an external content creator separately. The internally produced digital materials belong to the organization from the start, so no special consideration will need to be given to them beyond compliance with records laws. Externally produced donated content may have special clauses in the donation agreements that have specific requirements in the event that your organization is no longer able to steward these materials. Those requirements should be built into your exit strategy. Taking all of these factors into account, research other institutions that may have the resources and be willing to accept your materials into their digital preservation programs. You may reach an agreement with one institution or several. Have a plan in place for the transfer of the materials, and keep the plan up to date as circumstances change at your home institution and the potential receptive organizations. I hope that you never need to use your plans, but it is better to have these agreements in place at the start than to have entire cultural heritage or institutional collections disappear.

I hope, through this report, I have made digital preservation less intimidating and mysterious. Digital materials will be available in the future only through active effort, and therefore it is critical to move beyond decision paralysis and into active preservation efforts. The hardest step you will take in this journey is the first one. After that, it will only get easier because, as with so many other skills we learn, practice is the key to success. As you move along your digital preservation journey, you will gain more expertise and confidence. You will also cultivate colleagues you can lean on for advice, technical support, and shared resources. Collaboration, internal and external, is vital to success because the very nature of digital materials, ever-evolving and mercurial, requires more expertise and resources to preserve than any one person or institution could ever develop on their own.

Notes

Notes

Notes

Library Technology REPORTS

Upcoming Issues	
October 55:7	**Protecting Privacy on Library Websites: Critical Technologies and Implementation Trends** by Marshall Breeding
November/ December 55:8	**Blockchain in Libraries** by Michael Meth
January 56:1	**Digital Disruption** by Bohyun Kim